Poetry for Your Girlfriend and Hairless Cat

Deo-Mark Macadaeg

BookLeaf Publishing

India | USA | UK

Poetry for Your Girlfriend and Hairless Cat
© 2022 Deo-Mark Macadaeg

Presentation by *BookLeaf Publishing*

Web: www.bookleafpub.com

E-mail: info@bookleafpub.com

ISBN : 9789357445689

First edition 2022

DEDICATION

Dedicated to Em HarJo and Winston

Poetry for Emily / Poetry for Win

Keep these poems close to you
When u be feeling stressed
Your cat loves you and I do too
But he thinks I'm the best

Winston you are just a cat
But I swear you don't act like it
The demon hours you like so much
Are far from perfect timing

Now as for us, your human parents - not sure
who loves you more
All I know is you're worth much more than the
phone she traded you for

I'll keep writing poetry
To keep your heart with me
These words and letters are meant for you
While you work on your MD

I Can't See

Right eye 20/20
Left eye like 20 - one million

I have not a clue what the scales mean,
All I know is that I can not see

I mean I can see alright out of my right eye
But when its closed all depth perception is off

You saw me blow hot wax into my eye
And i think thats where it got lost

Youre my vision when the lights go out
And my vision when we're far apart

I dont need two working eyes
As long as i have your working heart

Mean to me

Jokes at your expense
To which you say,
"Mean to me"

The quote I think is funny -
If the jokes are not actually mean

If you make jokes at my expense
I'll clap back, as you have seen
But when you say the word "everything"
That's what you Mean to Me

I Need to Look at a Calendar

I Need to Look at a Calendar
Let's leave and lets go somewhere warm Em

Jamaica with your friends
And then Playa Del Carmen

We've got a plan
Maybe Croatia, Japan

Somehow Santorini
We'll play in the sand

Eggs

Tell me why at one point I used to like yolks
runny,
But now I can only eat yolks hard

You always liked eggs, like you like your jokes
funny
And like winston likes rolling in the yard

But whats not to like,
you like chia seeds and oats

I like my eggs scrambled
You like your eggs poached

you want them sooner than later
Before they become toast

We've got plenty of time
I know you don't have the most

But once you are ready
for eggs the way you want to

That's when I'll be ready
To have breakfast with you

Drunk

Drunk in Love
When Ben and Mitch said I do
We drank way too much
I drank more than you

We danced like your mom
And took jag to the head
I passed out on chairs
While you force fed me bread

I called my brother
To take both of us home
I let it all out that evening
Now I owe you a new phone

Not an ideal morning
We woke up soaking wet
But as far as weddings go
Now the bar is set

Stuck

Stuck in this dorm room waiting on the results
Results came back negative for COVID-19
Ninteen minutes later, I receive a text
Text message claims another passenger was not
as lucky as I

I sit there and wait til they say what to do next
Next morning I'm up and I hop into a van
Van driver says its 10 hours
10 Hours pass
Pass Dryden, Kenora, end up in Winnipeg

Winnipeg Airport Hotel, where we have to stay
Stay for 2 weeks
Weak is how i feel by day 7
Seven more to go

Go look at the planes
Plain ones I ignore those
Those military ones i like
Like yellow and black ones

One more day of quarantine, then i'll be free
Free from boredom, mostly
Most of all no longer stuck

Writer's Block

Why the fuck did i start this challenge
To be honest i thought it would be great
Something sentimental, from the heart
But i'm in this hotel room, with a massive
headache

I have no regrets though
It's called a challenge for a reason
You may call some of these poems "criminal"
A crime. Like treason

Some of these poems,
Are fillers like this one
But some of them are heaters
Like the underside of winston

Now the ball is rolling
I quite like this pattern
Why the fuck did i start this challenge
Because this poetry book matters

O.F.I.F.C.

Only Fella in First Class.
Seat beside me is empty.
Only one in this Row.
I wish it was you with me

I'll just grab another Molson
Unhealthy habits that get me through
Working extra on this MacBook
Wish I was chatting with you

This rotation different
I've dreamed of this work life now
And if you asked my 15 year old self
I know he would be proud

But the 17 and 2017 versions of me
Had some different priorities
And maybe he'd like this life
If he could do it affordably

(written on the plane)

We Dem Boyz

"Yeah ayy!
Yeah ayy!
Yeah, boyz
Yeah
Hol up, hol up
Hol up, we dem boyz
Hol up, we dem boyz
Hol up, hol up, hol up, we makin' noise, hol up
Hol up, hol up, hol up, hol up
Hol up, we dem boyz
Hol up, we dem boyz
Hol up, hol up, hol up, we makin' noise, hol up
Hol up, we dem boyz"

- Wiz Khalifa

whoops

I forgot that this is being published
Like every word of it
The serious poems start now
Please disregard the previous shit

SIKE

You thought this was different?
These poems may not reveal all of me
But one things for sure
They'll decrease in quality

I'm really pumping these out
I thought 21 would be feasible
The first ones were okay
But the rest aint gon' be readable

WINSTON!

Meow meowmeow
spspsps

Here boy
spspspspspspsps

Hi winston! Thank you for licking my hand
Ow fuck

Election Year

I'm not checking my phone
Not even once
This eve of the election
I don't want to know who won

As I enter this bubble,
I'll stay off of the twitter
Cause if i see who just won
I might become bitter

You're lucky you're just a cat
With one eye and no political beliefs
Not sure how you would vote
You just like when you get to eat

Wet food or dry food,
You lean to the right
But with parents like yours
We'll all be alright

Spis

formerly known as griffin
Aka the female sphinx
If he has the parasite
We do too, i think

He likes to go for walks
Well not walks, more like rolls
It seems he likes to cuddle
But I really just think he's cold

But I'll hold him anyways
And I'll walk on all fours
And pull back on his head
Because he's my son and yours

Prius Prime

You called it your dream car
Before you even drove it
40km all electric
You'll love it i know it

Ron Mack hasn't called
Be patient don't worry
It'll be here soon
We're not in a hurry

One day he'll call
You'll be eating your toast
Then we'll plan our trip
And drive to the coast

Lake of the Woods

Stopped for some chinese food.
On this drive that i'm bored of
A restaurant called "Yummy Yummy"
In downtown Kenora

Its take out only
Due to the restrictions
The combination plate looks as filling
As it looks delicious

I need somewhere to sit down
To enjoy my plate
I'll park in this Shoppers
Its facing the Lake

A thousand kilometers away
But there's familiarity to it
Could be the trees turning orange
Or the lake people's music

It's not my first time here
I'm sure i'll be here again
To eat the same sweet and sour sauce
That we'd get at Thiens'

What are u gonna be for halloween?

I'm thinking Spiderman and Spider-Gwen
Oh you don't think i'm serious?
Its as cool as Khal Drogo
If you are Daenerys

We were Chad and Avril a couple years ago
Look at this photograph
Last year we were e-kids
We gotta do better than that

You could be Dr. Evil
Bigglesworth played by Winston
I guess I could be Austin Powers
That Hit would be Instant

But you want to be Taylor
And then I'll be Kanye
We'll dress up like they did
And we'll make my house the VMAs

I'm okay with this idea
Seems fairly inexpensive
I hope the others' costumes are as funny
Not like Drew's - quite offensive

It'll be a good time regardless,
you in that sparkly dress
Myself with the henny
Hope I won't be a mess

Quilt

I remember you made a quilt
For your AP English poetry
Josh made a sweater
Jaime made a tree

He couldn't sew worth shit
Not as well as you do
To be honest, every project but yours
Was straight poopoo

You put in countless hours
I put in half a day
I think TPaz was buggin
We should've switched grades

Your quilts back then brought
Kindness, dedication, bliss
Your quilts today bring warmth
And a home to me and spiss

Home

City of Bridges
Home to West Side Dougie
The Paris of the Prairies
How did we get so lucky?

Half a century spent,
Between both you and me
Plus spiss makes it 50-something
How could we ever leave?

I've got so many memories,
of the fellas, pulling our pranks
You had a front row view,
So you fill in my blanks

Our families are here
This will always be our Nest
I love Saskatoon like I love you
I can't wait to see what's next

Home 2

[Page left intentionally blank for Me & Emily to write the sequel]

www.ingramcontent.com/pod-product-compliance
Lightning Source LLC
Chambersburg PA
CBHW070735160726
48003CB00006BA/2516